Malaga
City trip

A vitamin supplement to classic tourist guides, to consume without moderation!

Cristina & Olivier Rebière

Copyright © Cristina & Olivier Rebière

All rights reserved.

ISBN : 9798525995482

TABLE OF CONTENTS

Introduction	1
Practical tips	2
How to use the *eGuide*?	6
GeoNAV	8
PhotoNAV, IcoNAV	9
Province of Malaga	10
1. Malaga	12
2. Benalmádena and Fuengirola	29
Spain: general presentation of the country	41
Andalusian Gastronomy	43
Travel lexicon	45
Credits, Authors	48

Introduction

We welcome you to your new **Voyage Experience** guide: «**Malaga - City trip**». If you are planning to spend a weekend or a short stay of a few days in Malaga, then this guide will help you to discover this beautiful Andalusian city, located between the sea and the mountains.

If you want to go there for one or several weeks, then the guide: "Province of Malaga" in the same collection will be more suitable since it will allow you to discover this magnificent province of Spain, nestled in an exceptional natural setting. Bathed by the Mediterranean and the sun, this province is a real gem. It does not know winter along its coastline with its beautiful beaches (300 days of sunshine per year on average!!!). Malaga is also mountainous in the interior, where nature and its varied landscapes will surely charm you. Olive and almond tree plantations as far as the eye can see, white villages hidden in the heights of the hills or mountains, shiny remote valleys where the sweetness of life is not just a mere concept. We discovered this province during the Covid health crisis because Spain had the wisdom to reverse the first decisions made in panic.

While in several countries quarantines were the norm, in Spain, the management by autonomous regions allowed travel within provinces with open restaurants, museums and other leisure and cultural structures. We were fortunate to know the Spaniards in a different light and to appreciate their *joie de vivre*. While respecting the sanitary measures, we were able to continue to live normally, make visits and walks in nature.

We will share with you our discoveries: the beautiful city of Malaga, but also the picturesque Antequera, Nerja with its exceptional cave as well as other jewels that make this province of the *Costa del Sol* a destination to discover in any season. We have spent more than two months travelling through it and we will certainly return to it as it has conquered our hearts.

You can imagine that we do not have a team like the French *Guide du Routard* or Lonely Planet (and this is in fact not the goal of our approach), therefore you will not find in this e-book a full list of addresses of accommodation or restaurants. We share with you our journeys, our experiences. We hope this will help you discover new destinations and make you want to visit them.

If you own an Android smartphone and want to save on internet data transfer, use the free *MapFactor Navigator* app that we recommend WARMLY, tested and approved on roads around the world. The maps are free to download in order to enjoy offline mode and navigate without permanent connection.

This e-book or "e-guide" works almost like a website, but without a connection (unless you want to access the many hyperlinks, especially to "OpenStreetMap", that we propose during the book).

Bon voyage !

With kind regards,
Cristina & Olivier

Practical tips for Spain

How to get to Spain?

Depending on the country of origin, good deals can be different to get cheaper airline tickets. Here are some tips that may apply to your situation, regardless of where you travel from.

Buy your tickets in advance (minimum 3 months) to benefit from the best rates; if you have the possibility to choose the dates of your holidays, prefer those where there are promotions on the different airlines. Do not buy your tickets right away, but "test" the market first. Look for the airlines that fly to Spain: Madrid, Barcelona or Malaga here https://www.aena.es/en/malaga-costa-del-sol.html or in Seville. Buy your tickets first and secondly prepare your itinerary depending on this data.

Watch out for ticket prices that can vary from hour to hour, without apparent logic. Therefore, I advise you to save on your computer the prices of tickets obtained on different days, and after comparison, you can decide what o buy. This way, you can not only compare prices, but determine a trend and you will know when you will have "stumbled" on a price not to be missed. You can save more than 300€/ticket.

Avoid holiday periods if possible (Christmas, New Year, National Day, Holy Week, etc.) so that you can get the best prices for airline tickets.

Depending on your starting point, try the following airlines to increase your chances of getting good prices: **Alitalia, KLM, Iberia**, but also *lowcost* airlines like **Easyjet, Ryanair, Wizz Air, Blue Air**.

As you probably know, Spain is a very visited country, so tourists are present almost all throughout the year. The seaside resorts are crowded during the summer season, whereas cities with a strong cultural and artistic character such as Barcelona, Madrid, Seville or Cordoba are visited in all seasons.

Best period to visit: the spring and autumn months when there are few tourists. Temperatures are almost never negative and during the summer temperatures range from 20 to 35°C, but they can exceed 40°C if there is no sea breeze. On the coast of the eastern part of the province you will find a subtropical climate. The vegetation you will encounter will make you think of the Caribbean, while in the western part the Mediterranean climate is more subject to oceanic influence, with more abundant rains. Winters are short and mild, except in the north where they are colder.

How to move around?

Tips: Renting a car remains the most suitable means of locomotion if you want to visit the region in complete freedom. You can rent it at one of the airports if you arrive by plane, otherwise the roads are very good and you can get there easily by road. You can also get there by train or bus. This last variant is inexpensive and there are several bus companies that serve Andalusia like **Flixbus, BlaBlaBus** and **Eurolines**.

Attention: you must guarantee your car rental with a credit card. If you have not booked online with insurance included, you can have surprises once you are there because the bill can easily climb up.

Speed limits:

In Spain the speed limits are as follows:
- Urban area: 50 km/h.
- Rural areas, on single-lane roads: 90 km/h,
- "vía rápida" type roads : 100 km/h.
- On highways ("autopista") and fast lanes ("autovía"): 110 or 120 km/h.

Spain offers the great advantage of having a good network of free motorways in addition to the paying ones. Remember that an ***autovía*** is free while an ***autopista*** (signalized with AP) is paying. Often there is a paid highway and a free one with the same number, which tells you that they follow about the same route. Like the famous AP-7 (paying) and A7 (free) that cross several Spanish regions.

Requirement to have 2 pre-warning triangles (1 for the front of the car, one for the back), a fluorescent vest and a box of spare bulbs. Attention, you can get fines in case of absence in the vehicle.

Accommodation

There are several types of accommodation in Spain, from apartment rentals to hotels, hostels and campsites. It all ultimately depends on your budget and how many people travel together. For families with child(ren) or if you travel with several persons, the most economical option remains the rental of apartments. The price of this type of accommodation is lower than the prices of hotel rooms and starts from 35€/night for an apartment that can accommodate 4 people. We mainly rented apartments for at least one month and thus obtained more interesting prices. We stayed for a month in Riogordo, in the mountains: the climate is wetter in spring and the cold is more biting than on the coast. We adored Benalmádena where we stayed for 2 and a half months in a very quiet little residence, with a nice swimming pool and a beautiful garden. We found these accommodations through *Booking.com* even though we later rented directly from the owners. In any case, the owners are very reactive, which is very appreciable.

Catering

During your stay in Spain, you can discover in addition to its magnificent landscapes, the rich gastronomy of this country. Foodies or food lovers will be able to enjoy tapas, many specialties of delicatessen and stews, dishes of meat and fish, soups and exquisite desserts.

In Andalusia, all along the coast you will meet hundreds of terraces with the famous "skewers" of sardines (*espetos de sardinas*), fish and squid, braised in typical boats as you can see in the photo below.

BE Careful, the Spaniards do not eat at all at strictly at noon, like the French. For example, lunch is usually served from 1 pm, although some restaurants open earlier to adapt to tourists. In fact, in Spain there are many restaurants that stay open all day long and you can drink and eat tapas at any time. A real joy, because there is never need to hurry to find a restaurant when you are visiting...! There will always be a small restaurant to serve you a hot meal. If you want to avoid the crowds and not wait for a table to open, we advise you to eat at 1pm. It is really the ideal time!

For more details on the local cuisine and some typical recipes see the "Gastronomy" section at the end of the book.

How to navigate the *eGuide*?

You have already read tens of books or even tourist guides in your life. They usually have a table of contents at the beginning of the entry, an index or a glossary, a table of photographs at the end of the book...

The electronic version of this guide contains a lot of this information, but also has a bonus that will help you mobilize content quickly and intuitively and create your own reading mode: it is a digital and tactile book, a kind of website that does not require an internet connection. We have organized this guide in a classic way for those who want to read "normally" without asking metaphysical or methodological questions: those of you can jump directly to the part "locations". For the curious or the geeks, here are three modes of navigation that we offer. You can always go back in your readthrough using the "Back" button on your smartphone, tablet or computer touchscreen.

A horizontal menu bar with 3 icons at the top

Your "eGuide Voyage Experience" contains at the top of each page a horizontal menu bar with three "floating" round icons located on the right. They are called "GeoNAV", "PhotoNAV" and "IcoNAV". Their operation is explained below. All underlined texts are hypertext links or hyperlinks for short, so you can click them (on your computer) or press them with your finger (on your touch screen). You can see colorful, square thematic icons with a pictogram inside. Here are some examples:

These icons clearly and simply show you the interests that are present in the respective section. The background color of these icons depends on the theme. You can see the details of these icons in the chapter on IcoNAV.

Right at the top right, you see THREE navigation icons,

rather round, with a dominant black pictogram. Here is the detailed explanation:

1. GeoNAV: a "classical" geographic exploration

In the electronic version, by touching with your finger or by clicking the **hyperlink** located immediately under this icon of round shape with the stylized compass, you access a "classic" view of the map, with **colored geographical areas** and **hyperlinks next to the map** that allow you to access the respective chapter (a smaller geographical area of the general map). From there, you can select the tourist site that interests you.

2. PhotoNAV: discover the dream locations through photos

In the electronic version, by touching with your finger or clicking the hypertext link located immediately **under this icon** of round shape with a camera, you can discover the beauties of the country thanks to the **best photos** I made myself or even those made available on *Wikipedia* by the authors I credit and thank at the end of the book. So: if you like a photo, tap on it (or on the hyperlink immediately below) and jump directly to the respective touristic location!

3. IcoNAV: choose your interests by icons

In the electronic version, by touching with your finger or by clicking the hypertext link (or hyperlink) located immediately under this icon of round shape, completely to the right with a question mark on a black background, you access the list of all interests, or "icons", present in this e-Guide. In the chapter "IcoNAV", you can discover the themes of the icons and, for each of them, the list of touristic sites where this icon is found, in the form of hyperlinks that you can activate, by clicking or touching them with your finger. Nothing could be easier!

How to view geographic maps?

In the electronic version, if you are not connected to the internet and if your e-reader allows it, you can zoom (with your mouse wheel or with a two-finger pinch-to-zoom) on the maps embedded in the touristic sites (their resolution makes it possible to do so). If you are connected to the internet you can also access the maps offered by the site **"OpenStreetMap"** by clicking or pressing with the finger on the corresponding hyperlink (here circled with red) located immediately below the respective map.

GeoNAV

Browse your *Voyage Experience* eGuide by choosing your place of stay on the map areas.

Province of Malaga in blue, 2 tourist sections (in this guide)

Malaga

PhotoNAV

My favorite photos

Malaga   Benalmadena

IcoNAV

In the electronic version, you can browse the Voyage Experience eGuide by choosing the thematic icons of your interests or affinities.

"Voyage Experience" and general information icons

 COUP DE COEUR
Malaga | Benalmádena et Fuengirola

 TIP
Malaga | Benalmádena et Fuengirola

 CHILDREN
Malaga | Benalmádena,Fuengirola

 IMPRESSIONS:
Malaga | Benalmádena et Fuengirola

"Water" icons:

 BEACH
Malaga | Benalmádena, Fuengirola

 NAUTICAL ACTIVITIES
Malaga | Benalmádena, Fuengirola

"Culture" icons:

 ART-CULTURE Malaga | Benalmádena et Fuengirola

 MUSEUM Malaga | Benalmádena et Fuengirola

 RUINS Malaga | Benalmádena,Fuengirola

 ARCHITECTURE Malaga | Benalmádena et Fuengirola

 CASTLE Malaga | Benalmádena et Fuengirola

 RELIGIOUS MONUMENT Malaga Benalmádena,Fuengirola

"Nature" icons:

 **GARDEN, PARK** Malaga | BenalmádenaFuengirola

 **HIKE** Malaga | Benalmádena et Fuengirola

 **FAUNA** Malaga | Benalmádena et Fuengirola

LANDSCAPE Malaga | Benalmádena et Fuengirola

"Sport" icons:

 BYCICLE Malaga

"Leisure and life on site" icons:

 ACOMODATION Malaga | Benalmádena et Fuengirola

 RESTAURANT Malaga | Benalmádena et Fuengirola

 LEISURE PARK Benalmádena et Fuengirola

 SHOPPING, SOUVENIRS Malaga | BenalmádenaFuengirola

 BUDGET Malaga | Benalmádena et Fuengirola

Province of Malaga

The province of Malaga (in Spanish: *Provincia de Málaga*) is one of the eight provinces of the Autonomous Community of Andalusia, which is located in the south of Spain. Bordered to the south by the Mediterranean coast, the famous *Costa del Sol*, this

Andalusian province is located between the provinces of Granada and Cádiz and to the south of those of Córdoba and Seville. Its variety of landscapes, between sea, mountain, hills and valleys make all the charm of this region: wide undulating spaces covered with olive and almond trees, high peaks of the *Penibaetic Cordillera*, superb beaches with different coast resorts, or dizzying gorges.

Its capital is the city of **Malaga** which has witnessed the economic and cultural development of the western Mediterranean. The Phoenician *Malaka* had become at the time a prosperous trade region. After the Muslim invasion of the VIIIth century, its territory was later integrated into the Nasrid kingdom of Granada and experienced a new period of commercial and cultural golden age. By visiting this beautiful province, you will go from surprise to surprise!

Because there is something for everyone: coastline resorts spread over more than 160 kilometers of coastline, full of life, with very well-appointed beaches and sea walks lined with countless restaurants, cafes, pastries, shops and green spaces, from seaside resorts to flowery neighborhoods that will be appreciated by people enjoying quietness. But you will find other very lively ones with many shopping malls and attractions for all ages, then villages full of charm, unspoilt nature in around fifteen protected natural areas with forests and magical valleys sheltering foxes, chamois, golden eagles and many bird species.

The *Guadalhorce* river flows through the province from north to south, and in its western half, flow the *Guadiaro* and *Guadalete* rivers. The *Fuente de Piedra* lagoon is famous for its colony of flamingos and is also worth a visit.

1. Malaga   2. Benalmádena and Fuengirola

1. Malaga

Malaga is located to the west of the Mediterranean Sea, about a hundred kilometers east of the Strait of Gibraltar. It is the capital of the province of the same name. It is located 530 km south of Madrid. Ideally located in the center of a bay surrounded by mountains, it is crossed by two rivers: the *Guadalhorce* and the *Guadalmedina*.

Founded by the Phoenicians in the VIIIth century B.C. under the name of *Malakka*, Malaga is in fact one of the oldest European cities. In 573 BC, it passed under the control of the Carthaginians, then became Roman in -219 following the Punic wars. Thanks to its port, it was growing and was notably known for its exports of *garum* to Rome. Around 411, the city fell into the hands of the Vandals of King Gunderic, then the Visigoths of King Wallia took control of it around 416. The city would continue its eventful history by passing from the Byzantines to the Visigoths, then to the Moors and would even be pillaged by the Viking leader Hasting in 858.

Malaga is a tourist city that has retained its character over the years and its remains testify to its rich cosmopolitan past. We loved its beautiful seafront promenade - the *Paseo Marítimo*, with its beaches, lively terraces and shops of all kinds and also the modern harbor pier (*Paseo del Muelle Uno*) with its magnificent panoramic view of the city. Get lost in the pedestrian alleys of the old center, enjoy the shady squares of orange trees with bewitching fragrances, admire the vestiges of its history whilst enjoying its sparkling modernity: Malaga knows how to charm even the most extravagant visitors!

A map of Malaga with tourist locations to visit

I advise you to visit the capital of the province in the spring as we did because there are not many tourists and the city is very pleasant to travel into. If you are going by car, I advise you to park in the university area, near the *Plaza del Ejido* or in the streets *Calle Guillén Sotelo, Calle Carretería* because you can find free parking lots which is very convenient:-). You will be close enough to the center in order to visit everything on foot. In the historic center, you will find several maps with the tourist objectives of the visit that will help you to find those you are interested in.

Photo 1.1: panoramic view of Malaga from the *Paseo del Muelle Uno*

Head towards the beautiful *Plaza de la Merced* square with its central obelisk in memory of General Torrijos. Then you will see a beautiful tower in Mudejar style that belongs to the *Iglesia de Santiago Apóstol* church. Its style is a harmonious mix between Gothic and early Mudejar styles, with a Baroque touch from the early XVIIIth century. The artist Pablo Picasso was baptized in this church on November 10, 1881. His native house is to be found also on the square mentioned above. The Picasso Museum (number 11 on the map) is only a few hundred meters away, in the *Palacio de Buenavista* palace, in the *Calle San Agustín* street. You will find there many works by the artist and several hundred books on this great painter. For all the details about the museum and to buy tickets online, go to their website: <u>museopicassomalaga.org</u>.

14

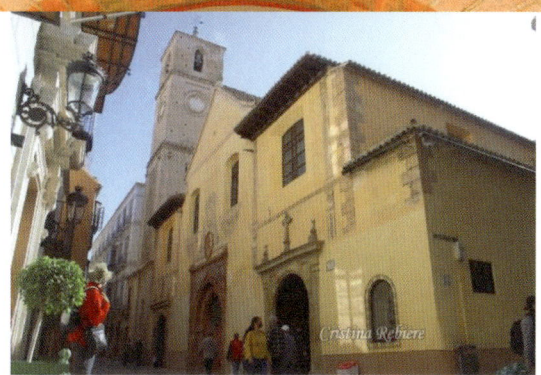

Photo 1.3: *Iglesia de Santiago Apóstol* church

Right near there is the beautiful pedestrian street **Calle Alcazabilla** going from Plaza de María Guerrero next to Plaza de la Merced to *Plaza de la Aduana* where you can admire the Customs Palace (*Palacio de la Aduana*) whose construction began in 1788. Its initial purpose was to assist the traffic of the port, which was intensifying at the time thanks to trade with the Americas. Located next to the beautiful Malaga Park, it currently houses the Malaga Museum. The history of the construction of this palace is eventful as it was interrupted several times because of the wars. In this museum are gathered the collections of the former Museum of Fine Arts and the Archaeological Museum of Malaga. European citizens enter free of charge and others pay a modest sum of 1.5€ as in many museums in Andalusia. In the central part of the *Calle Alcazabilla* the rear of the Picasso Museum can be found, with its tree-lined garden next to the Jewish quarter of Malaga and a small square - the *Plaza de la Judería* - formed around the Mudejar tower, which serves as a union with the *Calle Granada*. If you want to eat, have a drink or a coffee, enjoy an Andalusian pastry, nibble on a few tapas or go shopping, then do not hesitate to roam the nearby pedestrian streets. You will certainly have the choice to find what you want!

Photo 1. 7: Roman theatre and Alcazaba in Malaga

On the side closest to the slope that climbs to the Alcazaba, lays the beautiful Albéniz cinema, built in 1945 and which combines historical architecture with the Californian style of some American cinemas. Next to this building are the interpretation center and the ruins of the Malaga Roman Theater (number 3 on the map). It was discovered in 1951 after the demolition of the House of Culture, which occupied part of this space. In the middle of the street you can admire, under a small glass pyramid, the vestiges found underground, notably pits used to make the precious "garum", a fermented fish sauce.

The Romans used the natural slope on which the Alcazaba de Malaga is located to build the theater, whose access to the public can be found on the *Plaza de la Aduana*, where the *Palacio de la Aduana*, which we spoke about just before, is located. There is also a small garden called *Ibn Gabirol Gardens*, which houses a sculpture in tribute to this Jewish and Andalusian poet and philosopher. The interpretation center located next to the theatre is open to the public from Tuesday to Sunday, so you can browse the site through wooden footbridges. Nevertheless you can admire at any time the ruins that are visible from the square.

A large part of the bleachers is visible, as well as the orchestra richly decorated with large marble slabs, and the stage, in which today its pavement was reproduced with a parquet like that he would have had at the time. The scene closed at the back with an ornamental façade decorated with openings, columns and sculptures, several of which have been recovered. It was built according to the architectural model established by the Roman architect Vitruvio, and was used as a theater until the end of the IIIrd century. Then, a factory for the exploitation of salted fish and the production of sauces like garum was installed here and remained active until the Vth century, when the pools, some of which are still visible today were reused as burial places, turning this place into a necropolis. After the Muslim conquest in 711, a military complex and a mosque were built there.

Photo 1.9: Palacio de la Aduana

You can then either continue your visit towards the cathedral, or make a stop by the **Alcazaba de Malaga** (from the Arabic al-qaṣbah, قصبة, al qasbah, "citadel") which is a palatial fortification of the Islamic period, built on an ancient fortification of Phoenician-Punic origin (number **2** on the map). Located just above the historic center of the city, which was the ancient Madina of Malaqa, it is surmounted by the castle of *Gibralfaro* (number **4** on the map). This complex is an eloquent example of the military architecture of the Taifa period, of the XIth century, with its double enclosure and a large number of fortifications. Built between the XIth and XIVth centuries by the Moors, this fortified royal residence testifies to medieval times and Taifa malagueña. It is composed of several concentric walls guarded by towers. At present, access to the castle of Gibralfaro is made through open passages in the area of the barbican located next to the Interpretation Center. The sentry walk is located at the top of the walls and the barbican that completely surrounds the castle is preserved in excellent condition. Inside the castle, you can see the *Airón* well, 40 meters deep, cut in the rock and fed by a source that still exists, but also by a rainwater collection system through canals leading the water to several underground reservoirs, all covered with brick vaults.

The largest is in an octagon shape and emerges at the center of the fortress. Two bread ovens were preserved there, as well as several booths from different eras. The former powder magazine has been converted into an interpretation Center. After successive interventions, the wall contains currently thirty sections guarded by eight towers. The great *Torre Blanca*, in the form of a clog, was used as a prison at different times of its existence. It dominates the access door of the north slope closing the barbican and opening itself onto the curtain wall. It is an imposing chicane door, preceded by a space intended for guards, surmounted by a vault decorated with pendants with interlacing bricks and bicolored ceramics. The tallest tower is the *Torre Mayor* (Big Tower), located in the south-east, with its 17 meters of height. It was an autonomous fortified building with water supply, but also warehouses and living rooms. This was the best vantage point of the castle. You will recognize the beauty of a palace in Arabic style organized around rectangular patios with its gardens and water basins (*Patio de los Surtidores*, *Patio de la Alberca*). You can visit the archaeological museum which exhibits the remains found in the Alcazaba and which is sheltered in the palace. For all the details of the visit, see their website in English. You can buy a ticket either for the visit of one of the two sites or for both at the same time, at a more interesting price.

Photo 1.11: Access to the Alcazaba

Photo 1.12: Cathedral of the Incarnation of Malaga

You can then continue your visit towards the Cathedral of the Incarnation of Malaga (number **1** on the map). If you take the same route as us, you will first discover its rear part, then its magnificent baroque door. Built on an old mosque of which only subsists the *Patio de los Naranjos*, from the XVIth century, the construction works were interrupted in 1782. which undoubtedly earned it the nickname of "*La Manquita*" (the one-armed). It is harmoniously combining different architectural styles: Gothic floor, layout and bedside in Renaissance style, and its main facade and decoration of the door in Baroque style.

The north tower reaches a height of 84 meters, making it the second highest cathedral of Andalusia after the Giralda of Seville. The south tower is unfinished. The entrance for the visit of its interior in Renaissance style costs 6 € with the *Catedralicio Museum*, but you can admire it for free if you go there during the mass.

Photo 1.13: Hospital Santo Tomas Apostol

In the *Calle Sta. María* you can admire a superb building housing the *Hospital Santo Tomas Apostol*, a true architectural gem. Founded in 1504 during the conquest of the city by the Catholic monarchs by one of the noble knights of the time, *Don Diego García de Hinestrosa*, it was first a charitable institution. The building was greatly affected by the December 1884 earthquake, and construction of a new building began in 1888. The architect designed it in the historicist line, inspired by the Gothic-Mudéjar style, fashionable at the end of the XIXth century. The chapel nevertheless retains a wooden coffered ceiling dating from 1505. Its beautiful flared door has an ogival arch and archivolts supported by stone jambs is framed by an *alfiz* decorated with glazed tiles. The building had a sanitary use until the middle of the last century.

Following the street, you will reach the Constitution Square. The *Plaza de la Constitución* is the center of Malaga life since the Reconquest. It bore several names: *Plaza de las Cuatro Calles*, then *Plaza Mayor* and in 1812 it was baptized with its current name. Among the buildings that surround the square you will notice that of the *Escuela de San Telmo* and the *Casa del Consulado*, but also the octagonal tower of the church *Iglesia del Santo Cristo de la Salud*. The Jesuits settled in this area next to a hermitage dedicated to Saint Sebastian, whose small dimensions made it necessary to build a larger building. It is the work of Pedro Sánchez who designed it on an octagonal base in 1572. Its construction continued during the following century. Since the XVIIth century, the square has been home to the fountain of Genoa or Charles V, which comes in fact from the famous Italian city. Most of the cultural events in Malaga are linked to this square as during the Easter Holy Week, during the Malaga Fair, and during the celebration of New Year's Eve.

Photo 1.14: Constitution Square

It is also from this square that you can start shopping for the big brands that are located in the surrounding shopping streets.

You can then go and enjoy the freshness and beauty of the Malaga Park while admiring the beautiful buildings of the *Paseo del Parque*. The park extends from the *Plaza de la Marina*, in the west, up to *Plaza del General Torrijos* and to *La Malagueta*, notably the *Plaza de Toros* of the la Malagueta. It is a Mediterranean garden with many tropical and subtropical species, which make it one of the most important public parks in Europe in terms of exotic flora. Mixing the style of the Renaissance and Baroque gardens, botanical species from the five continents will amaze you, as well as the corners arranged in romantic style with typical decorations of the region like the benches covered with Sevillian tiles, sculptures and obelisks in memory of famous Malaga figures such as Rubén Darío, Salvador Rueda or the painter Antonio Muñoz Degrain.

The decor is complemented by the presence of fountains, such as the *Fuente de la Muñeca*, the *Fuente de la Ninfa* or the *Fuente de las Tres Gracias* located in the *Plaza del General Torrijos*. In the center of the park you will find the Eduardo Ocón Municipal Auditorium, where music festivals or other cultural events take place throughout the year.

Photo 1.17: Park of Malaga

Malaga

Photo 1.18: Ayuntamiento de Málaga

You can contemplate not far from here the beautiful building of the Malaga City Hall - *Ayuntamiento de Málaga* - and the *Jardines de Pedro Luis Alonso* garden, right next to the town hall, between the gardens of the *Puerta Oscura* and the park of Malaga. Named after the first post-war mayor, Pedro Luis Alonso, this Latin garden with Spanish-Arab and French influences is arranged in geometric lines. Orange and tangerine trees give a sweet smell to the air as they bloom. The colors of their fruits contrast with the deep green of cypresses, much of which has been replaced by rosebushes. As for the beautiful building housing the town hall of Malaga, also known as *Casona del Parque*, it is a XXth century building in neo-baroque style with modernist details, surrounded by the gardens of the *Puerta Oscura* and other emblematic buildings of Malaga such as the Bank of Spain, the *Palacio de la Aduana* or the Rectorate of the University of Malaga. A few meters away are the Malaga Bullring (*Plaza de Toros* - number **8** on the map), built in 1874 by the Spanish architect Joaquín Rucoba. Called *La Malagueta* because of the beach of the same name, very close, it is one of the symbolic places of the city of Malaga. For bullfighting enthusiasts, you can visit the

Antonio Ordóñez Bullfighting Museum. At Easter, the traditional *"Corrida Picassiana"* takes place, in which the bullfighter dresses with a costume inspired by the works of Pablo Picasso.

If you want to enjoy the beach, then this is where you will find one of the most famous and beautiful beaches of the city: *Playa la Malagueta*. Stretching on more than one kilometer, with a width of more than forty meters, it is a fine sandy beach bordered by the beautiful promenade that makes the round of the port. You will find restaurants there, cafes and shops for everyone's tastes. The beach is well equipped with showers, play areas for children and you can rent sun loungers, parasols and nautical equipment. In short, there is everything you need to spend a beautiful day with your family!

Photo 1.21: Playa la Malagueta.

Do not miss the *Paseo del Muelle Uno*, which is part of the *Paseo de la Farola* promenade, with shops, leisure area, restaurants and an underground parking lot of 1050 places, as well as a reception area for cruise passengers in transit.

The port of Malaga was chosen to host a representation in Spain of the Centre Pompidou in Paris. If you are an art lover, you will easily identify the "*Cube de Muelle Uno*" which houses the Centre Pompidou de Malaga, a museum with works of art offered by the great Parisian museum. For all the details, see their website here. The redevelopment of Pier 2 led to the creation of a recreational area: *El Palmeral de las Sorpresas* which includes a ferry terminal and a catering area.

Photo 1.22: Paseo del Muelle Uno.

If you are hungry, a visit not to be missed is that of the Central Market of Malaga: *Mercado Central de Atarazanas* which is located one kilometer west of Malaga Park. (number **9** on the map). Built in 1879, you will notice its impressive marble door from the Nazarie era when there was a naval workshop here, hence its name *Atarazanas* which means "arsenal". Renovated between 2008 and 2010, its glazing is superb, representing the monuments of the city and the stands of the market have a different color depending on the products sold: green for fruits and vegetables, orange for meat and blue for fish.

If you like the gardens (just like me) then you can make a small visit by the Botanical Garden of the *Concepcion* (number **6** on the map) which is located towards the northern exit of the city of Malaga, 3 km from the center, towards Antequera, at the edge of the highway. Created in 1850 by the Marquis of Loring and his wife, it includes more than 5,000 tropical and subtropical species, with water basins, fountains and waterfalls. Several itineraries of discovery are proposed to you in the garden like: the "Around the World in 80 trees", "The Plants of Our Earth" with typical plants of the region like olive trees, almond trees, vines, pomegranates, strawberry trees, oleanders, etc. For all the details regarding opening hours and price, go to their website.

Photo 1.26: Botanical garden of the Concepcion

If you want to stay and spend the night in Malaga, you can choose either a hotel or an apartment via Booking.com. You can have a double room with shared bathroom for 20€ per night – not in the middle of the city center – just like in the *Residencia Universitaria San José* which is 200 meters from the cathedral. By booking directly on their site you will even pay less than on Booking;-). You will find studios at about thirty euros and even apartments with 2 bedrooms for this price. If you prefer hotels, a good choice is the *Ibis Budget Málaga Centro* which is located in the center, 300 meters from the market and less than a kilometer from the train station and the Cathedral of Malaga. The price of a double room is a little more expensive than the previous options but depart from 44€. You can book on Booking or directly on the Accor website because there is no price difference.

Malaga

There are so many restaurants in Malaga that you will be spoilt for choice; seafood and fish, Andalusian specialties, but you will also find many Indian and Asian restaurants and many British or Irish pubs as there are many Anglophone tourists in this city. There are restaurants that offer menus at attractive prices around 10€ (*Menu del dia*) including an appetizer, a main course, a dessert, bread and drink. We ate in the city center, on a small square, where the prices were lower than those of the *Paseo maritimo*. No need to give you the name of the restaurant because there are so many to discover that it is better to let yourself be guided by your instincts and your desires of the moment. If you want good pastries and delicious coffee and chocolates, don't miss the **Granier** chain, a real favorite for us, with unbeatable prices and quality products. We adored their *Farton*, but also their chocolate, almonds and honey pretzels.

 For hiking and nature lovers, Malaga is also an excellent place as the Malaga Mountains surrounding the city offer striking landscapes between the bright green of the pine forests and the deep blue of the sea. The *Montes de Malaga* Nature Park, considered the green lung of the city, is easily accessible from the city. There are several hiking trails, of different difficulties, for all tastes and all ages.

An easy hike is the **Mirador del Cochino**, which is almost 7 km long and can be reached from Malaga by the A-7000 road, less than twenty kilometers north of the city. Its name is due to the pig-shaped sculpture at the beginning of the *El Cerrado* marked trail. With virtually no difference in altitude, it is a proper family outing even with children and an opportunity to admire beautiful landscapes and panoramic views of the city. If you take binoculars, you can admire the elegant flight of birds of prey such as the botted eagle or the short-toed snake eagle at the *Mirador Vázquez*

Sell which is at the end.

Finally, if you want to take more difficult paths, you have the choice in *Lagar de Torrijos* where you will find an eco-museum as well as a camping area built around an old wine press typical of the region. This is a cheap accommodation option for camping lovers. But be careful because there is a whole procedure to follow as you can read on the official website of Andalusia. In fact, on the site you will find plenty of information and several other hikes. In any case, you can visit the eco-museum to discover the ancient utensils used to make Malaga sweet wine, olive oil and bread. You will see an old oil mill and bread ovens for cooking the traditional "*cateto*".

One of the hikes that starts from here is *Torrijos of Chinchilla* which is an 8 km loop a little harder than the first, but it has its charm since it follows streams and you can admire there the presses and mills like the *Lagar de Santillana* or the *Lagar de las Ucemillas*. To start the hike, take the direction *Carretera de los Montes*, up to a small trail on your left with a chain. You will have to follow it to the left towards *El Mirlo* creek. There is also an easier trail that will last about thirty minutes through pine forests along Chaperas creek and its tributaries. Do not hesitate to visit the official website of the *Junta de Andalucia* which offers you a lot of information on everything there is to do in the region. For bike rides know that there are specially arranged routes, such as the medium-difficulty *Carril cicloturista de Lagar de Contreras*, whose starting point is near two flour mills built at the same time as the *Molinos de San Telmo* aqueduct. Just like ten other mills along the route of the aqueduct, which constitute one of the most important projects carried out in Spain in the XVIIIth century, the aim of which was to improve Malaga's water supply to the Guadalmedina river.

2. Benalmádena and Fuengirola

Benalmádena is a coastal resort about twenty kilometers south of Malaga, nestled just like the capital of the province in a superb setting between sea and mountains. It has a very rich history, even if its present aspect which is so modern could not be guessed.

The earliest known inhabitants of *Benalmádena* date from the Upper Paleolithic Solutrean period, some 18,000 years ago. During this period, a real explosion of population took place all along the Andalusian Mediterranean limestone arch, and sometimes inland. For Prehistory enthusiasts, we will give you some spots not to be missed near the city, but also even more within the guide of the **Province of Malaga**.

You can see some vestiges of these times spread through the city, although numerous ruins are not always easily identifiable as for example those of *Benalroma*, one of the archaeological sites of the Roman era with residential use and which underwent transformations from the IIIrd century AD. They are located at the beginning of the *Avenida de las Palmeras* after the intersection with *Avenida Antonio Machado* which runs along the beach. These ruins are protected by a brick roof and facade. There are no plates, but you can see them through the iron fence, closed with a large chain (see photo below).

Malaga

Photo 20: Roman ruins of de *Benalroma*

      Two favorite things in the same guide probably seems exaggerated to you, but the reality is that we really loved *Benalmádena*. This resort has everything to please: fine sand beaches, a long promenade by the sea - the famous *Paseo maritimo*, a superb marina straight out of the 1001 nights, hundreds of restaurants, cafes, pastries and shops both along the promenade that continues in fact in the nearby resort of Torremolinos (with less charm in its center). There are also neighborhoods with quiet residences with swimming pools for the most part and flowery gardens, singing birds, bougainvilleas and jacarandas that adorn the white walls with their bright colors, a city center with lively alleys, lined with typical Andalusian houses and then the old village "Benalmádena pueblo" located on the heights and just as picturesque.

We lived there for two and a half months – that is to say that we had plenty of time to change our mind and yet that was not the case. And we will certainly come back there. We lived in a small residence, named *Los Horizontes*, with a nice swimming pool as you can see in the picture below, near the beach Saint Ana (*Playa de Santa Ana*), but also from the city center. We paid on average 600€/month for an apartment with one bedroom, which is a very good price for Andalusia, but it was in spring so outside of the high season. It is a resort suitable for families as well as couples of all ages. For children, in addition to the play areas on the beaches, you have several attractions that we will detail below.

Photo 2.2: *Benalmádena* Marina

 After the marina you will find a small beach, *Playa de Fuente de la Salud*, then a longer one that continues in the neighboring resort, the *Playa de la Carihuela* which is part of *Torremolinos*. South of the *Playa de Santa Ana*, towards *Fuengirola*, there are other beaches that follow one after the other. You can get there by car because there are free parking spaces all along the road that borders them. You have for example the *Playa Bil-Bil*, *Playa Alonso* or *Playa de las Verdas*. You can rent paddles, pedal boats, surfboards and you can practice all the water sports you want. The waves are quite present on some beaches while others are protected by arranged coves, which make them excellent for swimming. Of course all along these beaches you will find restaurants that range from simple *chiringuitos* with their fried and barbecued fish and seafood to more elegant clubs and pubs, Indian or Asian restaurants that are more of a second line to the beach. Do not miss the Bil Bil Castle in the *avenida Antonio Machado*, by the sea, which will certainly attract you with its traditional western Arab architecture, painted in red with its minaret and its Nasrid stucco interior. The building houses a small museum of Muslim art. For history and museum lovers, this is an excellent place to visit! There is also a tourist office there.

Photo 2.3: Bil Bil "Castle"

If you want to go shopping or even discover the lively center of *Benalmádena*, then meet upa at the shopping axis of the city: *Arroyo de la Miel*! Yes, it means the "brook of honey" and even if the honey does not flow that much, the sweetness of living is certainly a factor. This is also where you can find the *Casa de Cultura* in a house with Andalusian architecture with an interesting patio around which lay the various outbuildings, including its meeting room and an exhibition room, as well as offices. Benalmádena's cultural programming includes music, theater, exhibitions and other cultural events. This information is available and displayed on a billboard just in front of the center. Know that if you want to eat cheaper menus (at 10€ the full menu of the day!), it is in the streets of the center that you will be able to find them.

Photo 2.5: Casa de Cultura Benalmadena

We made a passion for a chain of restaurants offering excellent Thai food, large and succulent salads at very attractive prices: **Pad Thai Wok**. You will find several in Andalusia - to easily locate them, go see their website. Their *pad thai* are succulent and really reminiscent of the original pasta we ate in Thailand, which is rather rare in Europe... You can choose your ingredients and compose your dishes and the service is always fast. Nearby you will also find the pedestrian street *Calle Blas Infante* that you can see in the photo and where you will find one of the cafes of the **Granier** chain that I have already told you about in the city of Malaga. You will find another one on the beach too, at the end of Torremolinos.

Photo 2.6: Pad Thai Wok Benalmadena

Photo 2.6: Calle Blas Infante with the Granier pastry

One of the largest parks in the city is the Park of the dove - *Parque de la Paloma*, located on the *Avenida de Federico García Lorca* with a large lake, ponds and fountains and tree-lined alleys. It includes a garden of cacti and other plants, play areas for children, but also several species of wild birds in freedom like ducks, swans, peacocks and even hens. Nearby there is the *Selwo Marina* dolphinarium and its colony of penguins that will delight the little ones.

To continue with the attractions that will enchant children and teenagers, but also adults who have kept their childish soul, *Benalmadena* offers a really good concentration at this level, bringing together several leisure parks. The most famous is **Tivoli World**, even though the Covid health crisis has hit it hard and thus is in great financial difficulty. You will find many attractions for all ages, from the most childish to the most dizzying, but also gardens, entertainment and shows for all tastes. For all the details and to see if it has reopened its doors, go visit their site. Another attraction that has remained open despite the crisis is the *Sea Life Benalmádena* which is located in the Marina of the city, just at the entrance, in front of the *Torre Bermeja* tower and next to the shopping center "Marina Shopping". In the 25 aquariums divided into 9 rooms, you will see more than 5,000 specimens from the Mediterranean, the Atlantic and the tropical zones of India, the Pacific, the Red Sea and the Amazon. A family outing that will amaze the children! You can see all the details on their website. If you have children, a little tip: buy tickets combined with the *Fuengirola BioParc* (of which you have more details a little below) because it will cost you less;-).

By taking the *Teleférico de Benalmádena* that connects the urban core of Arroyo de la Miel, near the Tivoli park, to the summit of *Monte Calamorro*, in the *Sierra de Mijas*, at an altitude of more than 700 m, you can see Africa's coastline on a clear day and you will contemplate beautiful panoramic views of the coast. With a length of more than 5,000 meters, it has become one of the most popular tourist attractions on the *Costa del Sol*. To get the details and even buy tickets combined with the amusement parks, go to their website. For hiking enthusiasts, you can walk some from the summit where the cable car takes you. A map with the trails can be found here **https://www.telefericobenalmadena.com/**. You can even ride your bike for a two-wheeled hike. For all the prices see their website.

At the top of *Monte Calamorro*, you can visit a pretty palace: *Castillo de Colomares*, built between 1987 and 1994 by Esteban Martín to pay tribute to Christopher Columbus and the discovery of America. It is a mixture of several architectural styles: neo-byzantine, neo-roman, neo-gothic and neo-mudejar. There is a chapel dedicated to Saint Elizabeth of Hungary, inscribed in the "Guinness Book of Records" as the smallest church in the world. What is interesting is that for its construction, a private initiative, techniques of the Middle Ages were used, without the help of machines, by Esteban himself with a couple of workers. If you want to visit it, know that Monday and Tuesday it is closed. For all the details, visit their site.

Photo 2.10: Mariposario de Benalmádena and the Stupa

Another attraction for all ages is the *Mariposario de Benalmádena*, located on the heights of the city, near the great *Stupa de Iluminación de Benalmádena* which can be seen from afar thanks to its golden tip. In this beautiful park, you will discover more than 1,500 butterflies flying freely from all parts of the world. More than 150 different species breed throughout the year in the park. Children will be able to discover all the stages of the fascinating life cycle of these wonderful creatures, from eggs to caterpillars and their bridal parades. You can even watch them hatch out of the chrysalis by witnessing their first flight after metamorphosis. The building is of Thai style, recalling very well the temples of this beautiful country. Moreover, the building materials and decorative elements were brought from Thailand. The choice of this style was dictated by the aesthetic harmony with the Buddhist temple located next to it, the Stupa of Lights that we cited. For all the details on prices and schedules, see their website.

Photo 2.12: Fuengirola beach

Right next to *Benalmádena* is another seaside resort of a slightly different style: **Fuengirola**. If in **Torremolinos** you can simply continue on the *Paseo Maritimo* to the north, this is not the case for Fuengirola where you have to go by car since it is about ten kilometers away. Along the coast there are beaches and hotels, resorts, etc. Parking spaces are free between the two resorts, but in Fuengirola all along its promenade, the blue spaces must be paid. Between 14:00 and 16:30, parking is free however. Throughout the beaches of this resort you will find equally varied restaurants. Even if we went several times to enjoy its walk and some restaurants like the Lebanese Casa Beirut whose specialties we greatly appreciated, the prices are more expensive. The sandy beaches are long and wide, with sunbeds and umbrellas for rent.

There are also several large shopping centers in the area. We really liked the **Miramar** in **Fuengirola** (exit 208A from the expressway) which offers many shops and a nice food court area with at least two restaurants that we tried with reasonable prices and where you can eat healthy: **Pad Thai Wok** which we have already told you about, but also **Pasapalo** (see their menu on their website), a popular family restaurant offering great South American and Asian specialties, salads and excellent desserts. Otherwise there is also the famous **Granier** and even **Starbucks** that we have left for the benefit of its Spanish competitors;-). There is also a large **Carrefour** supermarket which is convenient for buying the necessary food or something along those lines, a cinema with several theaters and even playgrounds for children.

Photo 2.14: Sohail Castle - Fuengirola

You can visit for free the Sohail Castle which is a fortress that was built in 956 by the Umayyad caliph Abd al-Rahman III on a rocky spur to ensure the defense of the coast. The fortress witnessed the Battle of Fuengirola in 1810. The size stones of the western foundations date from before the Roman era. For more details, on visit schedules, location, history and even to download an audio guide for your visit on your mobile, you can go here. You will also find details on the Roman site - *Finca del Secretario*, an archaeological housing complex stretching from the Ist to the VIth century. It is a city whose only thermal baths are known at the moment. It was reached by a monumental staircase with wall paintings leading to a distribution courtyard with a portico and paved with a polychrome mosaic with geometric motifs. Even more recently, you will notice the beautiful mosque of Fuengirola, built in 1991.

As we already mentioned, one attraction not to be missed with children (and even without!) is the *BioParc* of Fuengirola, a zoological park dedicated to tropical species and adapted to forest environments, notably Asia, Africa and Indo-Pacific islands. You will immerse yourself in the habitats of the animals, since this park has reproduced the living conditions of more than a hundred species among which are the dragon of Komodo, the pygmy hippopotamus, the tiger of Sumatra or the leopard of Sri Lanka. For all the details on prices and schedules, see their website.

For history lovers, you have at your disposal a beautiful museum to visit in Benalmádena: the *Museo de Arte Precolombino Felipe Orlando de Benalmádena*, located in *Benalmádena Pueblo*, on the *Plaza de las Tres Culturas*, which houses the pre-Columbian art collection of archaeologist Felipe Orlando with pieces from Mexico, Peru, Nicaragua, Colombia and Ecuador. Other contributions have transformed this museum into one of the best collections of pre-Columbian art outside of Latin America. It also contains an archaeological collection with pieces found in the municipality of the Upper Paleolithic at the Punic and Roman times. Check before you go if it is open because it is not always the case. The visit is free.

If you are in addition passionate of Prehistory like us,

Malaga

you will find nearby several spots to visit. It depends on how much time you have at your disposal. We have indicated in the guide "**Province of Malaga**" several superb itineraries with vestiges of rock paintings that you can walk onto, like us, and marvel at their good state of preservation.

As for the remains we were talking about at the beginning of this section, it is notably the *Cueva del Toro* which is the most important prehistoric site of the municipality since its discovery in 1969. Occupied and used as a sanctuary about 18,000 years ago in the Upper Palaeolithic Period, this cave is known for its cave paintings, including the one depicting a headless bovid. Located on Mount Calamorro, you can follow this route even if it is not marked, by downloading the route on Wikiloc. It is a fairly easy loop to make, accessible by the way of maintenance of the poles of the cable car. The cave is located on the east side of *Monte Calamorro* under a small wall that is today covered with graffiti, unfortunately. The 2-kilometer course still has some slopes representing more than 10% of elevation. It is therefore better to avoid doing this hike on a hot summer day. There are other more recent caves, from the Neolithic period, in the region such as the *Cueva de los Botijos*, the *Cueva de la Zorrera* and the *Cueva del Sahara*, whose vestiges are exhibited in the Archaeological Museum of Benalmádena.

Spain: general presentation of the country

Spain, in long form, the Kingdom of Spain, in Castilian *España* is a country in the southwest of Europe occupying most of the Iberian peninsula.

Capital: Madrid
Geography: Surface: 505.911 km^2
Population: around 46 million inhabitants.
Languages spoken: Spanish or Castilian is the official language throughout Spain. There are other official languages in some regions: Basque in the Basque Country and Navarre, Catalan in Catalonia, the Balearic Islands and the Valencian Community, Galician in Galicia, and Aranese Occitan in Val d'Aran.
Currency: Euro.

Infrastructure: The Spanish road network is highly developed with more than 346,000 km of roads including 9,000 km of motorway. There are toll highways, but there are also a lot of highways without tolls. The railway network contains more than 11,000 km and Madrid is connected by HST to several cities. Spain has more than a hundred airports and more than a dozen Spanish airlines serving their airspace. For all the details about transport in Spain see the Wikipedia article.

Climate: There are three major climatic zones in Spain: that of the Mediterranean climate in the south and north-west of the country, the oceanic climate in the west of the country and the semi-arid climate in the south-east which has a longer dry season than the summer.

History: The Iberians developed at the beginning of the Ist millennium B.C. which ended with the Roman conquest in the IInd century B.C. In the region that includes present-day Andalusia, around the basin of the Guadalquivir will develop the Tartessian culture, with a language, a writing, a culture and a social and political organization distinct from that of neighboring peoples, having a great Phoenician influence. From the XIIIth century BC, Celtic populations, known as the Celtiberian, began to gather in this Iberian settlement to the north and west.

From the IXth century BC, the Phoenicians created counters on the Mediterranean coasts. In 197 BC, the Romans divided the Iberian territories into two provinces: *Hispania citerior* to the north, with Tarraco (Tarragona), as capital, and *Hispania ulterior* to the south, with Corduba (Córdoba) as capital. After 63 and until the fall of the Roman Empire, Augustus Caesar founded several Roman colonies for veterans such as Caesaraugusta (Zaragoza). Vespasian (69-79) gave Latin law to all the cities of Hispania, allowing access to the Roman citizenship of the former magistrates of these cities and families of the Hispanic elite gradually integrated into the Roman imperial elite. The Latin language is the linguistic basis of most of the languages spoken today in the Iberian Peninsula.

At the fall of the Roman Empire in the Vth century, Germanic barbarians, the Suevi, Vandals and Visigoths invaded Spain. Until the VIIth century, the territory was inhabited by the Gothi (Visigoths) Hispanic-Roman natives (Hispani).

The Arab-Berbers led by Tariq ibn Ziyad conquered Spain in 711. In 756, Muslim Spain gained its independence and in 929, the country became a caliphate. In the XIth century, the caliphate fragmented into micro-states.

The political unification of present-day Spain began from the union of the Crowns of Castile and Aragon, through the marriage in 1469 of the heirs of these two states, the future Isabella I of Castile (1474-1504) and the future Ferdinand II of Aragon (1479-1516). In 1512, the Iberian part of the kingdom of Navarre was added and the Conquistadors began to conquer vast territories to form an immense colonial empire. The Spanish Inquisition, established in 1478 to maintain Catholic orthodoxy, fought against the «New Christians», conversos (former Jews converted by force) and moriscos, suspected of continuing to practice their original religions in hiding.

In the XVIth century, the Habsburg empire, of which the Spanish monarchy formed, together with the Holy Roman Empire, the essential element, became the first European power. In 1700, the grandson of French Louis XIV whose first wife was a Spanish infanta, became king of Spain under the name of Philip V, and founded the dynasty of the Spanish Bourbons, bound by the family pact to the Bourbons of France.

In 1808, Napoleon Ist invaded Spain and placed his brother Joseph Bonaparte on the throne. Spain lost most of its colonies in the XIXth century and a first republic was established. The Second Spanish Republic brought down the Bourbon monarchy in 1931. The extreme right (Carlists and Phalangists) organized an uprising, subjecting Spain, after a tragic civil war from 1936 to 1939, to the dictatorship of General Franco. Upon his death in 1975, the monarchy was restored and Juan Carlos I, the new king, quickly re-established representative democracy. If you want to know more about the turbulent history of Spain, see the article on Wikipedia.

Useful Websites

History, geography: Wikipedia - history of the country and for geography.

Tourism: An interesting site with a lot of information is here https://www.spain.info/en/.

For Andalusia, you can consult the website of the Andalusian Tourist Community in English here https://www.andalucia.org/en/home.

Andalusian Gastronomy

Andalusian cuisine is very rich in its multiple influences of peoples and civilizations who passed through this region leaving their marks in gastronomy. The Romans introduced olive oil, omnipresent in the cuisine of this region. The Arabs brought the dried fruits, the taste for vegetables, the mixtures of sweet and sour flavors and pastry. Side dishes and desserts have Jewish culinary influences. As for Christians, it is the use of meat that has been incorporated into the cuisine.

You can eat in tapas bars or on the terraces where there are often menus of the day, but also in more chic restaurants if you have a larger budget.

Appetizers and soups: The appetizers you can eat in all the bars, taverns and Andalusian restaurants are many tapas among which the **Salmorejo**, which is a cold cream like *gaspacho* made with tomato, bread and olive oil. A variant of *salmorejo* is served with ham and hard-boiled eggs and is then called the *porra*. Another cold Andalusian soup is *ajoblanco* made with grapes, garlic and almond.

The dishes: One of the typical dishes of Andalusia is the *Rabo de toro* which is a dish based on bull's tail, with onions, olive oil, tomatoes, peppers, garlic and carrots and spices. For the rest of the recipe see below. Fish are very much appreciated in Andalusia, notably the fried small fish, seafood, but also baked cod and all the possible and imaginable grills. Also try local ratatouille or breaded eggplants.

The desserts: There are plenty of typical Andalusian desserts among which you can taste the *Alfajores* (almond and walnut pastries), the *torta loca* (crazy pie), a Malaga specialty consisting of two disks of puff pastry with pastry cream covered with an orange glaze. This popular dessert is present in any Andalusian pastry shop. In Cadiz you can try the bread of Cadiz and the *gañote of Ubrique*. This bun is made of almond paste and stuffed with candied fruit and is also known as the *Cadiz turron*. As for the *gañotes*, it is a treat eaten especially during the Holy Week but you will also find it during the rest of the year. In the form of fried reed, this dessert is made with eggs, cinnamon, sugar, olive oil, sesame and lemon zest. In Cordoba, the traditional flagship dessert is the *pastel cordobés* (laminated with a stuffing of angel hair).

In order to travel while staying in your kitchen or extend your experience in Spain, here are some recipes to make at home and bring some Andalusian gastronomy home.

Salmorejo

- 4 ripe tomatoes, 6 slices of country bread, 3 hard-boiled eggs
- 2 slices of serrano ham (or equivalent), 2 cloves of garlic
- 1 tablespoon of vinegar, olive oil, salt, pepper

Crumble the bread. Put the eggs to cook and leave them about ten minutes after boiling. Peel the eggs.

Peel the tomatoes and mix them in a food processor. Add the garlic, 2 tablespoons of olive oil, vinegar and bread crumb. Add salt and pepper according to your taste and refrigerate for one hour.

Serve cold with ham and diced eggs. You can also eat this soup hot if you prefer.

Gaspacho

- 1 cucumber, 7 very ripe tomatoes
- 1 clove of garlic, 1 red pepper, 1 yellow pepper
- 2 green onions, some fresh basil leaves
- olive oil, 1 tablespoon of vinegar

Wash all the vegetables and basil. Peel the cucumber and cut it into pieces. Cut the peppers into large slices and the tomatoes in half. Peel the garlic and cut it finely, as well as the green onion. Put everything in the food processor and mix. Add the olive oil and vinegar. Place the soup in the refrigerator for several hours. Serve the soup with finely cut basil leaves.

Pestiños

- 500 g flour, 1/2 glass of white wine, sugar powder
- zest of half an orange, 2 eggs, olive oil

In a frying pan, put 3 spoons of olive oil and fry the orange zest for one or two minutes until it is well scented. In a salad bowl, beat the eggs and gradually add the flour, white wine and the oil with the zest. Mix until a fine paste is obtained. Spread it out and cut rectangles. Fold the rectangles in half and then crush the corners in such a way as to make small purses. Fry the *Pestiños* in very hot oil. Turn them after a few minutes. When they are golden brown, drain and sprinkle with powdered or glazed sugar.

Andalusian Ratatouille

An easy recipe to make.
- 1 green pepper, 1 red pepper, 1 yellow pepper, 1 zucchini
- 2 tomatoes, 1 eggplant, 2 potatoes, 1 onion, olive oil

Wash, peel and chop the vegetables. Fry the onion and peppers in a skillet over medium heat with olive oil. Add the eggplant, potatoes and zucchini. Once the vegetables are well cooked, add the tomato and a pinch of salt. If you have sweet paprika, add some too.

Bull's tail

- 1 kg of a bull's or beef's tail, 3 onions
- 5-6 potatoes, 2-3 artichokes, 2-3 carrots, 6 ripe tomatoes
- 2 cloves of garlic, 300 ml red wine, olive oil, flour
- 1 glass of cognac, parsley, salt, pepper

Remove the fat from the tail and cut into pieces. Season with salt and pass through the flour. In a skillet, sauté in a little oil on each side, then set aside. Wash, peel and cut the vegetables into pieces. In a saucepan, sauté the onion in olive oil. Add the tomatoes, carrots and garlic. Add the pieces of meat and flambé it all with cognac. Add the wine and 300 ml of water, cover and cook over low heat for at least one hour, stirring from time to time. In another saucepan, boil the potatoes and artichokes cut into quarters for about ten minutes. Place the potatoes and artichokes on the meat and cook another 20 minutes, over low heat, until the meat is tender.

Travel lexicon: Spanish

As I travelled around the world, I realized that in some countries, it is not easy to manage if one does not know the language and if the natives do not speak a foreign language. I thought then that a small lexicon of "travel" would be very useful to you, not only to be able to be courteous (say Hello, Thank you, Goodbye), but also to know what to order in the restaurant. So I hope that my little travel lexicon will be useful to you so that you can manage during your trip!

Politeness and essential words/expressions

Hello! - **¡Buenos días!** (read as: buenos dyass)/for the afternoon **¡Buenas tardes!**
Goodbye! - **¡Hasta luego!** or **Adios** (adyoss)
Good evening! - **¡Buenas noches!**
Please - **Por favor**   Excuse me - **Perdona**
Yes – **sì**   No - **no**
Thank you - **Muchas gracias** (muchas grassyass)
How are you? - **¿Qué tal?**
Do you speak English? **¿Habla inglés?** (habla ingless)
I don't understand – **Perdón**
I don't know - **No lo sé**
Sorry – **Perdón** Excuse me (as in "sorry coming through") -**Con permiso**
Hospital – **hospital**   Pharmacy - **farmacia**
Bank – **banco**   Supermarket - **supermercado**
Street – **calle**   Doctor - **Médico doctor**

If you want more expressions and to hear the pronunciation, here is a free site https://ielanguages.com/spanishphrases.html where you can do it.

I preferred to write a "clean" phonetic transcription because the official phonetic signs are not always easy to remember;-), but you can also hear the pronunciation on the site above.

Malaga

Restaurant

Menu - menú or carta   To eat - comer
Breakfast - El desayuno
The addition please! - ¡La cuenta por favor!

Drink – bebida	Water – agua	Wine – Vino (byno)
Beer – cerveza	Bread – pan	Salt – sal
Pepper –pimienta	Mustard – mostaza	Soup – sopa
Salad – ensalada	Meat – carne	Pork - carne de cerdo
Beef - carne de res	Poulet – pollo	Fish – pescado
Seafood – mariscos	French fries - Patatas fritas	
Vegetables – verduras		Rice – arroz (arross)
Pasta – pastas	Sausages/Wieners -salchichas	
Potatoes – patatas	Cheese - queso	
Dessert – postre	Ice cream - helado	
haricots –frijoles	orange juice -zumo de naranja	

Bon appétit! - ¡Buen provecho!

At the hotel

Do you have available rooms? -¿Tiene alguna habitación disponible?
double room -habitación doble
simple room -habitación individual
bathroom -cuarto de baño
shower -ducha
What is the price for one night? - ¿Cuál es el precio de una noche? (cual es el pressyo deh una noche)
Can I see the room first please? -¿Podría echar un vistazo a la habitación, por favor?
clé - clave (clabeh)

Numbers

0 –cero	1 - uno	2 -dos
3 -tres (tress)	4 -cuatro	5 -cinco (sinko)
6 –seis(seyss)	7 –siete(syete)	8 –ocho
9 -nueve (nuebeh)	10 – diez (dyess)	11 -once (onsseh)
12 -doce (dosseh)	19 –diecinueve (dyessynuebe)	
20 -veinte (beynteh)	21 – veintiuno (beyntyuno)	
30 -treinta (treynta)	40 -cuarenta	50 –cincuenta
60 -sesenta (sessenta)	70 –setenta	
100 –cien	1000 –mil (like a mill)	

On the road and in town

Parking -estacionamiento   Train station -estación
Airport –aeropuerto   Bus -autobús
Train – tren   Day return ticket - Billete de ida y vuelta

Gas station -Estación de servicio   Entry -entrada
Exit –salida   Attention -atención
Prohibited –prohibido   carry on straight
ahead -recto
Turn left -Gire a la izquierda
Turn right -Gire a la derecha
Toilets -baños   How much does it cost? - ¿Cuánto cuesta?
It's too expensive! : Es demasiado caro

HOW TO GET THE EBOOK FOR FREE

Did you appreciate this paperback ?
Would you like to have an electronic version of it, for free ?
You could then have it on your smartphone, electronic reader or Kindle, always at hand!
It is easy: just send me an email with a proof of your purchase (this paperback) and I will send the file right away, into your inbox! For that, simply use my email address: cristina.rebiere@gmail.com
Hoping to read from you soon☺

Cristina

Credits

We would like to thank the sites Wikipedia, OpenStreetMap and open.mapquest.com for the resources used in the development of this book (photographs, maps and routes). We are grateful to all the contributors of these sites without which we could not have completed some of our articles. Thanks also to all the charitable souls who offer on the internet free tools and resources of use for those who always want to learn and improve!

Authors

Cristina & Olivier Rebière met at the age of 17 in 1990 in Romania, shortly after the fall of the Berlin Wall and the Romanian Revolution of December 1989. After two years of correspondence and several meetings, Cristina was able to get a scholarship to study in France and became Olivier's wife in 1993.

Since then, these two "life adventurers" have had an existence full of twists and turns, during which they fell in love with travel, entrepreneurship and writing. Their books are useful, practical, and will fill you up with energy and creativity. In addition to your practical guides of this collection, discover other ebooks here https://www.OlivierRebiere.com

Printed in Great Britain
by Amazon